Save Our Stream!

Text by Colin Polsky, Ph.D.
and Jane Tucker

Illustrations by Julia Miner

Lanham • New York • Boulder • Toronto • London

Published by Muddy Boots
An imprint of Globe Pequot
MuddyBootsBooks.com

Distributed by NATIONAL BOOK
NETWORK

British Library Cataloguing-in-Publication
Information available

Library of Congress Cataloguing-in-
Publication Information available

ISBN 978-1-63076-322-0 (hardcover)
ISBN 978-1-63076-330-5 (e-book)

Printed in China

About the Long Term Ecological Research (LTER) Network

The LTER Network is a large-scale
program supported by the National Science
Foundation. It consists of 28 ecological
research projects, each of which is focused on
a different ecosystem. The goals of the LTER
Network are:

Understanding: To understand a diverse array
of ecosystems at multiple spatial and temporal
scales.

Synthesis: To create general knowledge
through long-term, interdisciplinary research,
synthesis of information, and development
of theory.

Information: To inform the LTER and
broader scientific community by creating well-
designed and well-documented databases.

Legacies: To create a legacy of well designed
and documented long-term observations,
experiments, and archives of samples and
specimens for future generations.

Education: To promote training, teaching, and
learning about long-term ecological research
and the Earth's ecosystems, and to educate a
new generation of scientists.

Outreach: To reach out to the broader
scientific community, natural resource
managers, policymakers, and the general
public by providing decision support,
information, recommendations, and the
knowledge and capability to address complex
environmental challenges.

This material is based upon work supported
by the National Science Foundation under
grant no. DEB 1624129. Any opinions,
findings, and conclusions or recommendations
expressed in this material are those of the
author and do not necessarily reflect the view
of the National Science Foundation.

Acknowledgements

Many thanks to the students who made this
book possible, especially Abby Kaminski.
We are grateful to Dr. Anne Giblin for her
remarkable patience and assistance, and to
Dr. Diane McKnight, Amy Rinehart, and
Liz Duff for their leadership. The underlying
research was supported by the National
Science Foundation through grant numbers
OCE-0423565, -1058747, -1238212, and
-1637630, SES-0849985, BCS-0709685, and
EF-1065741, and by the Clark University
Human-Environment Regional Observatory
(HERO) program.

Dedication

*To all the professional and citizen scientists,
students, and teachers, who work to understand
the natural environment and our role as humans
in it.*
~CP & JT

*To my sister Tam — for giving me a home away
from home by the water — and her husband
Rick, for sharing his brilliant understanding of
all things natural.*
~JM

Annie bounds down the stairs in the morning. "It's a beautiful day! Let's go out and play!"

Her brother takes a quick bite before Annie drags him outside.

"How about some soccer?" Bradley says.

"You're on!" she replies.

1

Bradley passes the ball to Annie and she shoots it between two trees.

"Hey, can you two find another place to play?" their father asks.

"Why?" Bradley asks.

"I have to mow and fertilize the lawn. If the grass grows too tall, then you won't be able to run around easily," their dad says.

"But you hate yard work," Bradley says.

"True — but what would the neighbors think if we didn't take care of our lawn?"

Annie and Bradley set off to find someplace else to play.

What Lives in a Lawn?

What would happen if Annie and Bradley's dad and Mr. Chou didn't fertilize their lawns or treat them with pesticides? Their lawns would look a little different, but they would be healthier and much more interesting! A natural lawn has a mix of grasses and other plants, like clover and even dandelions. A lot of people work hard and pay a lot of money to get rid of dandelions, which are actually helpful, pulling needed calcium from deep below the surface. Without calcium in the surface soil, there are fewer earthworms. With fewer earthworms, the birds (such as robins) and animals (such as toads) have less food. Dandelions are also an important source of nutrition for honeybees. In the lawn food web, plants produce leaves, flowers, and seeds that provide food and shelter for animals. Bits of dead leaves and flowers fall to the ground where worms in the soil eat them, and fungi and microbes decompose them. These activities release nutrients and keep the soil loose. Plant roots grow down into the soil to get those nutrients, as well as water. Deep roots help plants to grow strong and more able to survive drought, diseases, and pests. Healthier plants mean more food and shelter for the insects and birds!

4

"Mr. Chou's yard looks like the soccer field at school. Maybe we can play here," comments Bradley.

"Howdy, kids," Mr. Chou says with a wave.

"Your yard is the greenest on the block," Annie says. "Can we play here?"

"Not right now. You see those flags in the ground?" Mr. Chou asks. "The chemicals those men sprayed yesterday could make kids or pets sick, so you need to wait a few days. The fertilizer is what makes my yard so green. The herbicides and pesticides get rid of the bugs and weeds," he proudly continues. "Sorry, you'll have to go somewhere else."

Disappointed, Annie and Bradley continue down the street.

"What are you two doing on such a lovely day?" their neighbor, Mrs. Riggio, asks.

6

"We're looking for a place to play," Bradley explains.

"Unfortunately, you can't play here. I have the sprinkler on to water my grass. I don't want your shoes to rip up the muddy ground. Maybe you can go play by the stream," Mrs. Riggio suggests.

"That's a good idea. Let's go, Bradley. I'll race you!" Annie yells, running down the street toward the stream.

7

Bradley jumps over the murky stream and watches an empty water bottle catch in a side pool before slowly meandering downstream.

"I can't tell if there are any creatures in here. It's all so green . . ."

Annie slips off her sneakers and dips her toes in the slow-moving water, "And slimy, too. Gross!"

Bradley looks closer. "I don't understand. Where are the minnows? Where are the frogs and the bugs?"

Suddenly, Bradley and Annie hear a splashing sound behind them.

What Lives in the Stream ?

Annie and Bradley notice that there's not much life in their stream. What's missing? Healthy ponds and streams contain many different life-forms that depend on each other to live — from single-celled algae to tiny floating duckweed to tall rooted cattails growing along the water's edge. These plants form the base of the aquatic food web because they are able to make their own food using energy from sunlight. Small plants and bits of larger plants become food for small animals, like dragonfly larvae and juvenile fish. Plants also provide shelter for small animals, who hide among their leaves from larger fish and other animals who want to eat them.

Startled, they turn around to find their neighbor walking through the water, wearing big rubber boots and carrying a box of test tubes and other equipment.

"What are you doing here, Ms. Carson?" Annie waves excitedly.

"I'm taking water samples from the stream," she explains.

"Why?" Bradley asks.

"Well, I'm an aquatic ecologist. It's my job to test the health of our local streams and rivers."

"This stream doesn't seem very healthy," Bradley notes.

11

Annie scoops up a handful of green slime from the water.

"Maybe this has something to do with why the water seems so empty,"
Annie says.

"That's part of it. We call the slime algae. It's a bunch of tiny plants. It's a clue as
to why we don't see much life in here. Let's see if we can figure out what's going
on in this stream."

Ms. Carson hands both kids a test tube, which they dip into the water. "When I add these special chemicals to the water, it will change color to show how many nutrients are in the stream," Ms. Carson says.

"Whoa! Mine is turning pink!" Bradley exclaims.

"And mine's turning dark blue!" Annie shouts.

"Unfortunately, dark colors mean there are a lot of nutrients. Pink means there is nitrogen and blue means there's phosphorus. Even though you might think lots of nutrients would be a good thing, when there are too many of them in the stream, they can cause the algae to grow too much, which makes it difficult for the fish to breathe."

Water Testing

We can test stream water to find out how many nutrients it contains. When special combinations of chemicals are added to a water sample, they react with the nutrient we are testing for. The reaction causes the water to change color in proportion to the amount of nutrient—the more nutrient, the darker the color. After a specific amount of time, the final color is compared to a reference chart to determine how much of the nutrient is in the water, and whether there is too much. A similar test can be used to measure the amount of oxygen in the water, so we can make sure there is enough for the fish and other animals to breathe.

"Where do the nutrients come from?" asks Annie.

"The nutrients in the stream could be coming from the grass fertilizer people put on their lawns," Ms. Carson explains. "We've also found pesticides from lawns in the stream, which kill the bugs that fish and frogs eat."

"We're losing our minnows and frogs because they don't have oxygen or food!" Bradley exclaims.

"Why would people put fertilizer and pesticides in the stream?" Annie asks.

Ms. Carson smiles. "They don't do it on purpose. When it rains, some of the water runs off of the ground and travels downhill into streams, taking with it some of the fertilizers and chemicals people put on their lawns."

15

Watering Regulations

Some communities have policies or rules that require people to water only on certain days of the week, or at specific times of day, such as late at night when it is cooler, so less of the water meant for the grass is lost to the sky through evaporation. Rules such as these are called *mandatory outdoor water-use restrictions.* Other policies give suggestions about lawn watering, called *voluntary outdoor water-use restrictions.* These rules can be made by cities, towns, or homeowners' associations.

WATER RESTRICTIONS IN EFFECT

16

"Does the same thing happen when we use our sprinklers?" Bradley asks.

"Yes. The more water we put on our yards, the more likely it is that we'll see fertilizers and chemicals run off into the stream," Ms. Carson answers.

"I get it. The ground is kind of like a sponge; if it gets too much water, it gets full, so the water has to run off somewhere," Bradley says.

"Exactly. Sooner or later, the runoff from all of the lawns goes to the same place: water—either the pond, the stream, or underground," Ms. Carson says. "That's important, because some people get their drinking water from underground." "So we should never put extra water or chemicals on our lawns?" Bradley asks as the trio heads back home.

"Well, a little bit doesn't hurt, but if your neighborhood applies a lot to its lawns, that can really affect the health of the stream, how much drinking water we have, and the food web on the lawn itself," Ms. Carson replies.

"We've got to do something!" Annie says.

"Maybe if we let our neighbors know what's going on, we can save the stream," Bradley suggests.

"Great idea. You'll need to convince people that they don't have to use so many chemicals on their lawns," Ms. Carson responds. "I know one person who said she wants to grow flowers and vegetables in her yard, like I do, but she thinks her neighbors wouldn't like it. Maybe the grown-ups will understand better if they hear the ideas from you kids."

Back at home, Bradley and Annie pull out some paper and markers.

"Let's mark the places in the neighborhood that might be affecting the stream," Annie begins.

"The sprinkler in Mrs. Riggio's yard was running all morning, and she wasn't even watching it!" Bradley says.

"Let's mark her yard with a blue circle," Annie says.

"Remember the warning flags in Mr. Chou's yard? Ms. Carson said that water from sprinklers can cause chemicals to run off lawns and into streams," Bradley says.

"Let's put a red X on his lawn," Annie declares.

"The Smith family lets their lawn grow naturally, so we can mark them with a green triangle," says Bradley. "And Ms. Carson changed her lawn to a vegetable and flower garden, so her yard gets a green triangle, too."

"What about the fertilizer Dad puts on our lawn?" Bradley asks. "It might be running into the stream and making the algae grow."

"Oh, no," Annie groans. "Put a red X on our lawn, too."

2

As the entire neighborhood gathers for the annual summer picnic, Annie climbs up on top of one of the tables.

"Hear ye, hear ye, friends and neighbors! We have some important news to share with you!" she calls.

"The stream at the bottom of the hill is in trouble," Bradley says, handing out copies of their map to the crowd. "The bugs and fish are disappearing."

Mr. Chou is intrigued. "What's wrong with the stream?"

"Well, it has to do with how we take care of our yards," Bradley explains.

"Really?" Mrs. Riggio asks.

"Yes. Putting too much water and chemicals on them can make the streams polluted, so minnows and tadpoles can't live there," Bradley responds.

"I guess I never thought much about it, but that makes sense," Dad agrees.

"And if we put less of those chemicals on our grass, the stream will be cleaner and healthier!" Annie cheers.

Then she whispers to Bradley, "And we might also be allowed to play in their yards."

23

Soon the neighbors start taking care of their lawns a little differently than before.

Mr. Chou uses fewer chemicals on his lawn.

Mrs. Riggio only waters her grass when the town regulations say it is okay, and never when it's raining.

Benefits of Natural Lawns

When we work too hard to have lawns with a single type
and color of grass, we disrupt the way the plants and animals and
microbes depend on each other. When we apply pesticides, the animals
and microbes living in the lawn and in the soil are killed, nutrients aren't
produced, and the ground becomes hard. Roots don't grow down to reach
water and nutrients, so the lawn then needs more water and fertilizer than
it would if it were left to grow more naturally. Therefore, maintaining an
unhealthy lawn can cost more than maintaining a healthy lawn.

The benefits of keeping a natural lawn are:
- You will use less water;
- You will use fewer chemicals (fertilizer, herbicides, pesticides);
- You will create more resilient plants better able to survive drought,
  disease, and pests;
- You will reduce runoff of chemicals to streams and ponds;
- You will attract birds, butterflies, and other wildlife;
- You will support beneficial and endangered insects, like honeybees;
- You will reduce lawn chores;
- You will provide a safer playing surface; and
- You will save money.

And as for Annie and Bradley's dad, he uses much less fertilizer than he did before.

"Hey, let's play some soccer," he calls to the kids. "I don't have as much yard work as I used to!"

27

The following year, the neighbors hold their picnic down by the stream, which is healthier. It has plenty of minnows, crayfish, and frogs.

"I know the stream is healthier, but I didn't think I would like the lawns if we put less stuff on them," Mr. Chou comments. "I was wrong; I love my lawn this way!"

"I love watching all of the birds enjoying my yard!" Mrs. Riggio adds.

"Here's to Annie and Bradley! You've done such a great job helping us strengthen our neighborhood. It just goes to show—even the smallest acts can make a big difference!" Ms. Carson cheers.

Glossary

Algae:
Aquatic plants that do not have roots, stems, or leaves. Some algae are so small they can only be seen under a microscope. Others may grow into long strings or thin sheets.

Aquatic Ecologist:
A scientist who studies all of the plants and animals living in an aquatic habitat (like streams, ponds, or lakes) and the way they interact with each other and with their environment.

Fertilizer:
Chemicals applied to lawns, gardens, or crops to provide nutrients for plants to grow. The key components of fertilizers are nitrogen and phosphorus. Chemical fertilizers contain large amounts of both. Compost may also be considered fertilizer. It contains nutrients beneficial for plants and soils, but contains lower amounts of nitrogen and phosphorus.

Food Web:
The interconnections and feeding relationships among a group of microbes, plants, and animals living in a particular habitat—in other words, a description or diagram of "Who eats whom (or what)."

Herbicide:
Chemicals used by people to kill weeds in lawns, gardens, or on crops.

Microbe:
Another word for microorganism, meaning a single-cell organism too small to see without using a microscope. The most familiar types of microbes are bacteria and single-cell types of algae and fungi. Microbes are found in air, water, soil, on us, and inside us! Although some microbes can cause diseases in plants and animals, most are beneficial. For example, without microbes in the soil, organic matter wouldn't decompose, nitrogen wouldn't be converted to nitrate, and plants wouldn't grow. Without microbes in their guts, animals (including people) could not digest their food.

Nitrogen:
Used to make proteins, nitrogen (symbol N) is essential for all living things. Nitrogen is present as a gas, as the largest component of the air we breathe. Elsewhere in the environment it is combined with other elements to form compounds that plants can use to grow. When nitrogen combines with oxygen it forms nitrate, a favorite of plants. Nitrate in the environment comes from the decomposition of organic matter. Nitrate is also a key ingredient in fertilizers.

Nutrient:
Any substance that provides nourishment to an organism for growth or for energy. Plants get their nutrients from substances dissolved in water or found in air, which they take up through their roots and leaves. Animals get their nutrients from plants and animals they eat.

Organic Matter:
Organic matter is a is a term that encompasses a wide variety of living or dead plant and animal material.

Pesticides:
Chemicals used to kill pests that eat or otherwise harm grasses or plants in lawns, gardens, and crops. Although pesticides are meant to kill harmful insects, slugs, or caterpillars, they also kill beneficial and harmless insects.

Phosphorus:
Used in genetic material and in energy-carrying molecules, phosphorus (symbol P) is an element essential for all living things. Phosphorus in the environment may come from the breakdown of organic matter or may be leached from some rocks. Phosphorus combines with oxygen to form phosphate. This is the form that plants can use, and is a key ingredient in fertilizers.

Test Tubes:
Small, cylinder-shaped vials made of clear glass or plastic with an open top and rounded bottom. Test tubes are used by scientists to hold small amounts of material for laboratory testing or for experiments.